Mind Travelers

Mind Travelers

Portraits of Famous Psychics
and Healers of Today

Loretta R. Washburn

For information write:

Hampton Roads Publishing Company, Inc.
891 Norfolk Square
Norfolk, VA 23502

Or call: (804)459-2453
FAX: (804)455-8907

If you are unable to order this book from your local
bookseller, you may order directly from the publisher.
Quantity discounts for organizations are available.
Call 1-800-766-8009, toll-free.

ISBN 1-57174-004-X

Printed on acid-free paper in the United States of America

—— DEDICATION ——

This book is dedicated to my three beautiful daughters, Shelly Peabody, Heidi Fruchtenicht, and Gerda Gartner. A special thank you to my soul sister, Arianne Wing-Miller, who supported and encouraged me from the idea of this book to its completion. Most of all to Curtiss Albany, who got up in the middle of night to solve all of my computer tribulations without any complaints—you are my friend, my love; you are the man who makes my heart dance.

TABLE OF CONTENTS

Introduction	9
A Contribution	19
A Tribute To Paul Solomon	21
Kenna Akash	25
Lynn Andrews	27
Sherri Evans Bolling	31
Celeste	35
Sandra Dolan	41
Elaine Eagle Woman	43
Patricia Hayes	47
Jananda	51
Kathy Lawrance	55
William Lawrance	57
Jeanie Loomis	61
Lin David Martin	63
Robin Miller	67
Robert Monroe	71
Kathy Oddenino	75
Rinatta Paries	77
Foster Perry	81
Sally Perry	85
Mary Reagan	91
Pat Rodegast	93
Kevin Ryerson	95
Mother Sarita	99
Gordon-Michael Scallion	103
Sandi Staylor	105
Dr. Robert Van de Castle	109
Walden Welch	111
Judi West	115
Zolar (Donald Papon)	119
Robert Zoller	123
Directory	127

── INTRODUCTION ──

It all started with Sherri Bolling, of Fair Oaks, California. Every Wednesday afternoon, on her television talk show "Look Who's Talking," she discussed astrology and numerology. People in the audience would give her their birth dates and she would tell them things going on in their lives, and what to look for in the coming. As I watched her, I knew that I was going to be her photographer and close friend. Eventually I made an appointment with her for a reading, and, sure enough, I became her photographer, close friend, and student.

Before meeting Sherri, I had been studying psychic awareness and picking up any book that I could find on metaphysics. With Sherri I explored further by taking several courses and then went on to take classes with another friend. I continued to study with Sherri and became a spiritual counselor.

Sherri was perpetually involved in some kind of fund-raiser, such as events for AIDS research and March of Dimes telethons. There was always something, and there I would be for her with camera in hand. She was quite the celebrity, and I had a lot of fun working with her. One of these events, to raise money for a new psychic development school that was about to be opened, was a dinner with Kevin Ryerson. Sherri was the hostess of the program and introduced Kevin, who is the most famous trance channel in the world today. After dinner, Kevin trance-channeled for everyone. The three entities that he channels came through and spoke to the audience about the world's spirituality, where we've been, and where we're going; then the entities answered questions from the audience.

A couple of months later, Kevin returned to Sacramento for another fund-raiser for the school. Again I was there with camera in hand.

Some time later—about five years, after I had moved to Connecticut and then here to Virginia Beach—it was time for me to get a reading from Kevin. I called to make an appointment, had the necessary paperwork mailed to me and returned, and arranged a time to talk with Kevin and receive my reading via telephone. I had dozens of questions for him, of course, but there was one in particular I needed answered. I had thought about writing this book for quite some time, and I wanted to see what Kevin would tell me about it in the reading. He thought that it was a good idea and that it would be successful.

Having already started the book, I decided to fly to California to photograph Kevin. (It was quite a ways to go just to photograph one person; it's not like Virginia is just around the corner. But I went.) With my best friend Arianne Wing-Miller, I met with Kevin and took his portrait, and then the three of us went to a little cafe around the corner from his office. Kevin provided enormous help for my book; he gave me a list of people that I should include, and told me where everyone was located. What he didn't tell me was that many of these people are like nomads; hunting them down was a job in itself.

While I was out west on this trip, I visited Sedona, Arizona. Although at first glance this side-tale may seem irrelevant, the experience and the many surprises I met helped to form my commitment to gather the photographs and information for this book while contributing to my personal growth. And so I ask that you indulge my wandering into my experiences in Sedona.

Sedona is one of the most spiritual places in the world, with a community of metaphysicians of all sorts. Alone and not sure where to begin, I decided that the first thing I should do is go to one of the vortexes and meditate, or do whatever it is that people do when they go to one of the vortexes in Sedona. I did a little research and decided that I wanted to go to Boynton Canyon, hike up to the top of the vortex, and see what would happen. As I started to climb, I felt a heaviness in my chest, and I heard a loud, high-pitched sound, like electricity. I suddenly had a severe headache from the sound. A couple of hikers passed me; I asked them if the sound was bothering them, but they had no idea what I was talking about. Then I realized that I was tuning in the electrical energy from the vortex. As I continued to climb, the heaviness in my chest increased, as though I were being crushed. I really didn't understand it; I only knew that I couldn't go any further. I sought a place to stop, get myself centered, and meditate. There was a flat rock sitting on the edge of the hill which looked like a good place for me to plant myself, so I took a seat, closed my eyes, and began to meditate. I had my chin down, when an energy pulled my head back and my eyes opened. I couldn't believe what I was seeing. Suspended in the air about six feet from me was an extraterrestrial. He smiled and began to communicate with me, not through words spoken aloud, but mentally. He didn't really say very much; he told me to have faith and trust what I feel, and that there would be more communication with me at different times. It didn't surprise me because I had many UFO experiences, but I had never spoken to any of them. When it was finished talking to me, it withdrew backwards at a high speed, and within just a couple of seconds, it was out of sight.

The next day I was scheduled to meet with William Lawrance, a medicine man. Before I left him, he told me that a couple of weeks before this visit, Spirit came to him and told him I was coming and he was to give me something. He makes beautiful medicine pots out of the rich Sedona clay, and he was told to make one for me and to give it to me. On most of his pots, he paints animals or Indian designs, whatever Spirit directs. Incredibly, the pot that he made for me had an extraterrestrial painted on it—and it looked just like the one I had seen at the canyon! I really wasn't sure what to make of it. I guess it made me a little nervous, a little intrigued, and awestruck. It was only later, after I met a few more people included in this book, that it made some sense to me.

A few months later, my daughter Heidi and I drove to California, stopping along the way to meet with people included in the book, and combining some visits with family and friends with business. With my friend Arianne, I headed back to Sedona—my second trip there, very different from the first.

I had read about the happenings that occur there, and I was anxious to experience some of that magic. Well, sure enough, the evening that we got there and headed up the mountain to Sky Lodge, I was driving slowly and to the left of the road was a creature of some sort. I thought it was a gorilla. This hairy body was rather hunched over and, as my lights hit him, he turned toward me; his face was that of a primitive man. We made eye contact, then he ran up the mountainside.

Logic dictated that it was a gorilla, yet it was definitely a man looking at me. Then better common sense set in—there are no apes in Sedona, Arizona. I later found out that Big Foot sightings are very common in this part of the country. Needless to say, I just knew he was going to come and get me in my sleep.

After Arianne and I checked to the lodge, we prepared ourselves for a big experience. Anyone who knows anything about Sedona knows about the UFO activity around here. Camera crews from all over the world come to tape the happenings, and movies are made about true personal experiences of dealings with extraterrestrials here. And after my last experience, I wanted more, and I wanted to share this with someone. So on this trip, I wanted to see something. I wanted to experience some of this; I wanted a taste of Sedona.

We headed up to Boynton Canyon with blankets and pillows, parked the car, and strategically placed the pillows on the windshield, so we could lie on the hood, rest our heads on the pillows, be comfortable, and have a panoramic view. It was dark out, yet the sky was filled with what looked like brilliant diamonds. As we lay there waiting patiently to see something earth-shattering, nothing seemed to be happening. Then we realized that those little diamond-like images in the sky were moving. Moving, not about the sky, but in little square designs. Every once in awhile one would travel, or move over to another light and blend in with it, as if it becoming one with it. We took turns yelling, "Did you see that!" About every ten minutes a flash of light would dart across the sky. No, these were not shooting stars; they simply traveled across the sky making sharp turns or simply shot up into the sky. Some were green, some blue, and some red, and they left tails of light behind. We were there for a couple of hours and wanted to stay longer, but the cold chased us off. Besides, we had stayed until midnight, and our travel-weary bodies had to get some sleep. We were satisfied—we saw about a hundred different activities.

I wished for more time to explore. After two days of work, however, I had to deliver my fellow-explorer Arianne to the airport in Phoenix and meet my daughter Heidi's plane. Despite living in her mother's metaphysical world, she was my biggest skeptic. I told her all about what Ar and I had experienced and wanted to know if she would like to check it out. She didn't really want to, but she did it to humor me.

I took her to the same place, and we saw about fifty different activities in the sky, but she watched from inside the car. I guess she was afraid something was going to get her. The following day we climbed the rocks at Boynton Canyon and meditated and experienced some of the beauty of the place together.

Sedona is a magical kingdom; wonderful things happen to people when they're there, and I can't wait to get back.

Fresh from the enthusiasm and commitment to the book that Sedona gave me, I proceeded to schedule the rest of this enormous project. And wondered what I had gotten myself into. I met with challenges all along the way. I would make appointments with people and travel great distances to keep those appointments, and they wouldn't be there. Or the weather would be uncooperative. Or something else—always something. I guess it was a lesson to see how strong my will was. . .or something, I'm not sure. I only knew that I was not going to let anything get in my way.

My plan to see Patricia Hayes, at Delphi in McCaysville, Georgia, is an example of the challenges I encountered. I had been told that it was only a six- or seven-hour drive from Virginia Beach. That didn't seem so bad. Heidi was taking a break from school, so again I dragged her with me. After a drive of twelve hours, we were there. With several photo shoots scheduled for the next day, I couldn't even spend the night. I was with Patricia for a few hours, hopped in the car, and drove home. I was so tired that I took a wrong turn, got lost, and got home thirteen hours later, just in time for my first appointment. To top it off, I don't do snow, and it had started snowing on my return home.

The rest of my trips were relatively small, with the exception of my journey to New England. I flew to Rhode Island and was met by my friend Elaine King. It just happened to be during the big storm of January '94—not just a storm, the Big Storm. We had snow, freezing rain, and icy roads to contend with. Elaine was a sport and, in spite of it all, I got almost all of my work done. We managed to get to New Hampshire, Connecticut, New Jersey, and New York City. The only place that I was unable to reach was the Cape. I truly wanted to get Rob Hand, a master astrologer, in the book, but the weather didn't allow. I decided to take an early flight home because the weather continued to worsen, and flew out just hours before the airport closed down.

A few days after this trip, I had my second meeting with Sally Perry, a medicine woman. I was scheduled to go to a sweat lodge ceremony that she was doing. I was so inspired that the following day I sat down and wrote about her and my experience in the sweat. In the section about Sally Perry I also mention a handsome man by the name of Curtiss Albany. What I didn't share in that section is that healing and magic truly happen in a sweat; not only that, but love came into our lives—yes, the two of us found what true, unconditional love is all about, and he is now my fiancé.

And so, with my readers' indulgence, I wander again in my telling of how this book came to be because all these things are part of why and how I gathered these people together within a book's pages. Curtiss and I live together in a beautiful log cabin nestled in the woods. The energy here is very strong, and from the beginning I knew that there is UFO activity here. This is a large vortex that we are sitting on. After I brought this realization to Curt's attention, we lay in bed one night, feeling as though we had company, looking out the window. There they were. We had visitors, who communicate with us and visit us quite often. It isn't alarming or frightening; I have had these experiences all of my life. They have even done some research with us; for example, I have three implants—in the back of my neck, in my shoulder, and in my arm—for easier communication with them. One night my daughter woke up with her room lit up. When she looked at the foot of her bed, there stood an extraterrestrial holding her foot. When she let it know that she was frightened, there was a smile from this being, and then it simply disappeared. Sometimes I feel as though my life is just a big wonderful adventure, and I'm just here for the ride. Maybe that's what a lot of it's all about. I was told by Sherri Bolling that, while writing this book, I would find love from a man who is my equal spiritually. Sure enough, here he is.

Now, back to business here. A couple more small trips, and she was done, finished, through. No more traveling for me for awhile unless it's to some exotic place to lie in the sun. Well, she—the book—wasn't really done. I had hours upon hours to spend in the dark room, and then there were hours of unscrambling my notes and tapes and hammering away at the computer.

Originally the idea was to put together a book of famous metaphysicians for the general public. People get readings and spiritual counseling every day, but not everyone out there is necessarily all that spiritual or even psychic; many have other intentions. What I mean is that not everyone claiming to heal and be spiritual is working in a healing and spiritual way. Not, however, that to be good one must be famous; I'm certainly not saying that. Not everyone wants to work on the scale of the people in this book. But my goal was to provide an opportunity for people to know and perhaps contact the cream of the crop. Or simply be able to look at the portraits of these people and to read about them. Unfortunately, because of time and distance, omitted from this collection are gifted people who should be included. Maybe I'll do a sequel.

After completing the photography for the book I realized that it will also serve in another way as well. My readers will perhaps contact these people to learn from them as well as to use their services. In the '80s, people wanted the service of psychics, mediums, astrologers, and so on. Now, in the '90s, people want to learn to do these things for themselves. They want their spirits and souls to become one with the universe, to ask their higher selves and receive their own answers. To learn astrology, to do one's own chart. To learn how to channel. To heal oneself rather than going to a healer, since in actuality we heal ourselves and can be guided and taught to accept that responsibility for ourselves. People want to take care of themselves rather than allowing others to do so.

Everyone in this book lectures, does seminars, and has retreats. Some have their own institutes where you can go and stay to study. Many of them have their own books. As they share their personal experiences, we learn from these experiences. Many of their books are how-to books. Everyone in these pages wants you to claim your own spiritual self and travel on your own spiritual journey.

Through writing this book and meeting all of these people, I have grown so much—emotionally, mentally, spiritually, and physically. I have gone through some amazing healing and self-awareness. One of the most important things that has happened, is that when I now approach people, I approach them in a different manner. When I speak to people, I speak more deeply, to their souls. I have learned to become more understanding and forgiving, a more gentle creature of the earth.

I discovered quickly that I am unable to merely objectively and detachedly report about these gifted individuals. Getting to know them and experiencing their gifts in the process of getting information *about* them had an impact on me and tore down the reporter's wall of objectivity. But then I hope that makes the telling better because then my readers will feel as well as hear about each person within these pages.

The world is changing and I hope that you all meet with your own physical and spiritual quest. That you can all connect universally in mind, body, and soul. When those elements are in balance with one another, not only will you find a difference in your inner life, but you will find that you can create a better place to live and a career that is more in touch with who you are and what you truly enjoy doing. The personal expansion that can be achieved is limitless. We choose better relationships, have a better sense of self-worth, and grow in more positive ways.

Find out what's going on out there. Go to the medicine man or woman, enter a sweat lodge, explore a medicine wheel, or get didged. Get your astrological chart done. Get yourself healed and learn how to heal yourself and those around you. Go to a retreat, seminar, or lecture, or schedule one of these people to come to your community to speak. Use their services. Sit with a trance channel, or call one for a reading via telephone. Get your soul portrait drawn. Find out where you've been, your karmic lessons, and where you're headed.

Above all, remember: heaven is on earth!

—— A CONTRIBUTION ——

If one is to use this book, one is to enlighten herself or himself to truth beyond the physical realm. To put away all fears, expecting guilt and negative thoughts of oneself, and become enlightened to the possibilities that can be going on now and that which is yet to come. If you are ill, to know that you are ill because that is the state which you choose. If you are sad and lonely, that has been your choice; and if you are guilty or feeling unworthy, you alone have made these choices.

We are composed of three elements: BODY, MIND, and SPIRIT. If they are not all in sync with one another, all of these elements are considered to be ill. We are made up of energy. Energy creates energy. We must learn to create and accept love within ourselves and then we can learn to love one another. We need to eliminate negative thoughts so that we can create the life that we truly desire.

If we can learn to love ourselves and let go of the ego among us, we can gain a healthy BODY, MIND, and SPIRIT.

Remember that our bodies are simply instruments, and, like all instruments, we want to keep them in fine tune.

We must open our minds to gathering wisdom from life experience and receiving truth from Spirit. Then we can look at life in a different way. We can see that our bodies aren't just here for the time and then will die, but look at life in a way that our spirits gather experience and will go on to other lifetimes for those spirits are never dying.

If you are ill, do you want to learn how to heal yourself?

Do you want to learn to love yourself? Do you want to learn to pass through the gateway of your conscious mind? Do you want to see the choices in life that are most optimal to you? Do you want to see where you've been? Do you want to learn how to let go of fear? Do you want to see how your life today relates to other lives that you've lived? Do you want to know why you are the person that you are today and why you attract certain people, happenings, or thoughts?

The people listed in this book can guide you to a better understanding of who you are.

> Rhea
> Channeled by the instrument
> Loretta Washburn

— Special Tribute To Paul Solomon —
Trance Channel
Founder of
The Fellowship of the Inner Light

Meeting up with Paul Solomon wasn't the easiest thing to do. He lived right here in the same city as I, and was the toughest to catch. I would call him to make an appointment and he would be in Japan. Two weeks later, I'd try again; he'd been home but was now off to Thailand. I would say that this went on for about a year, when one day, when I had just about given up hope, I got a call from him asking me if I still wanted him for the book. Eager to get it while the gettin' was good, I scheduled to see him the following day. I sat with him listening to his stories about his work and his travels, learning what an incredible man he was. He made me laugh and he made me cry.

Less than a week later, I received a phone call from a friend telling me that Paul Solomon had passed away. I felt a need to include him in the book just the same, as a special tribute to him. His dedication to the children of the world was astounding. Paul traveled all around the world setting up orphanages for children who had been sold or simply kidnapped. He searched for and took these children back, endangering his own life for the freedom of the children. He cared for them, giving them a home, food to eat, medicine, and, most of all, love.

Paul Solomon founded The Fellowship of the Inner Light, in Virginia Beach. His work was often linked with a concern

for individual creativity and a drive for greater spiritual awareness.

This man has been acclaimed by audiences the world over as one of the most dynamic teachers in the modern movement of human potential. His lecture tours took him to Europe, the Middle East, Australia, New Zealand, South Africa, and Japan, as well as every major city in the United States.

In 1990, Hampton Roads Publishing Company published his book *The Meta-Human*, which is now in its second printing. Additionally, his gifts to us include the following books:

The Paul Solomon Tapes
A Healing Consciousness
Earth Changes and The New Planet Earth
Quest, Notes From a Student
  of The Mystery School
Twice Born
The Meta-Human
Feed My Little Lambs, a Manual For Parenting
Talk To Yourself—On Purpose!
Love and Fear, Only Two Powers Exist
The Tao of Communication
Be Emotional—and Love It!
Restaging Your Life in Three Acts

Paul, you are gone now, but your spirit will forever remain in the hearts of those you have touched!

—— Kenna Akash ——
Trance Channel

The magical land of Sedona is filled with many intuitives and healers of all kinds, but there are only a select few whom I have chosen for the book, and in this small group is Kenna Akash.

Kenna is a trance channel, channeling the entity Rojdnan. When I asked Kenna exactly who Rojdnan is, she said, "Rojdnan is an energy of love and he shows us how to alter our own perceptions and to live with more love in our lives. Universal love speaks through him. He teaches about self-empowerment and teaches you to be your greater teacher, inspires you to go beyond fear and discover your own potential. Get past the fear to know that you can do anything and that is what Rojdnan is there for."

Kenna used to work with The Psychic Friends Network, the one you see on television with Dionne Warwick. She gave psychic readings for them, and she now does psychic readings for her own phone line. She has always given personal readings in person or by telephone, with her readings being influenced by Rojdnan. Kenna channels mainly for large groups. It's interesting—Kenna sits quietly in a chair preparing herself with eyes closed, allowing Rojdnan to enter. Her eyes open wide, and she slaps her knees, standing and walking from one side of the stage to the other, with Rojdnan giving his words of wisdom, both tenderly and gently, along with much humor. He always has his audience laughing, and yet at the same time speaks so eloquently. He is truly a poet.

Kenna is putting together a book together of his prose. I would like to share with you some of his thoughts.

Love is the magic that you create with and life is the magic wand.

Laughter is a real key ingredient—finding the humor in life.

True love is letting go and allowing freedom, and to say *I allow you* is to say *I love you.*

Innocence is the part of you that does not question—it merely accepts.

Allow each obstacle to become a gift and experience an expression of your love.

How many ways can you paint a picture?
How many colors can a flower be?
How many ways can a branch grow on a tree?
Endless numbers of ways?
How many ways can I say to you, *I love you?*
Endless numbers of ways.

Kenna offers private readings and travels to channel Rojdnan for large groups.

Light Beams is a company selling greeting cards with Rojdnan's poetry and spirit bags. Kenna's husband makes small bags, and Kenna fills them with essence, according to individual needs. Your need could be anything from strength, to love, to forgiveness. These spirit bags can be ordered directly from her.

—— Lynn Andrews ——
Shaman
Author

My favorite city in the world is New York City, and trips there are exciting because I get to do the city, get some work done, and also visit my oldest daughter Shelly, who lives in Long Island. As I was preparing for such a trip, I learned that Lynn Andrews would be on the Island for a book signing. Thrilled, I grabbed opportunity while she was a-knocking. It was a real good thing that I did because later, when I went to California with hopes to see her, she was in Arizona; then when I got to Arizona, she was back in California.

My daughters and I went to the bookstore to meet this woman empowered by shamanic wisdom. Lynn read some lines from *Medicine Woman*, talked about her medicine cards, and spoke a great deal about menopause. I went home feeling more in touch with the woman and the little girl in me.

I read her books in the order in which she wrote them, beginning with *Medicine Woman,* which was a best seller and was later made into a movie for television. She followed that book with *Flight of the Seventh Moon,* one of my favorites; then *Windhorse Woman,* which truly captured my heart; *Crystal Woman; Jaguar Woman; Shakkai: Woman of the Sacred Garden;* and *Star Woman.* She also wrote *The Power Deck*, a series of self-affirming meditation cards, and two workbooks, *Teachings Around the Sacred Wheel* and *The Mask of Power,* a personal growth guide that helps readers discard their false masks or selves. To date, her newest book

is *Woman At the Edge of Two Worlds: The Spiritual Journey Through Menopause.*

Lynn's work began with a search for a more spiritual way of life, a way of healing herself and helping to rid the world of pain. In search of a spiritual teacher, she met two Native American women, Agnes Whistling Elk and Ruby Plenty Chiefs, and became their apprentice in the study of the ancient and sacred power of women.

Lynn works primarily with her mentors, Agnes and Ruby. She has also sought the counsel and wisdom of many other teachers from the Sisterhood of the Shields, a world-wide society of shaman women. Her books tell of her quests, which have taken her to Yucatan, Australia, Nepal, Tibet, and Japan.

Lynn Andrews lives in Los Angeles, where she spends much time in writing, providing shaman training to private clients, and spiritual healing—counseling privately. She also maintains and spends some time in a studio in Santa Fe, New Mexico. When she isn't traveling, she offers workshops around the United States as well as an annual intensive retreat in the high desert of Joshua Tree.

To get the full meaning of what Lynn Andrews is teaching the world, I read all of her books in the sequence that she wrote them. I found that by knowing her through her books, I learned to know myself—that was the true gift from Lynn. I also use *The Power Deck* almost daily. I find that these cards help me to center myself.

After listening to Lynn speak and reading her books, I've been able to look at myself in a different light. I have learned to love my body and my spirit. With my blood, I have produced a family, and now understand that soon I will cross the bridge, as Lynn puts it, into the world of wise blood, meaning that a woman retains her blood (her power) and her wisdom.

Books Available:
Medicine Woman

Flight of the Seventh Moon
Jaguar Woman
Crystal Woman
Windhorse Woman
Woman of Wyard
Shakkai
Woman At The Edge of Two Worlds
Mask of Power
The Power Deck

Counseling:
Spiritual Healing and Private Counseling

Retreats:
Annual Joshua Tree Retreat

Sherri Evans Bolling
Clairvoyant Astrologer
Numerologist
Spiritual Midwife

Sherri and I go way back. I first heard her on the radio and saw her on many television talk shows. Later, I received readings from her, and in time I became her personal photographer, and she my teacher. I took every class that she had to offer, worked with her, and became friends with her.

We first worked together at a time when I was known for going into buildings or homes that were so-called haunted and working as a light walker. Some called me the Sacramento Area Ghost Buster. When one of the Sacramento newspapers decided to do an article on a restaurant with strange things such as objects moving in the air, people walking around dressed in early-1900 clothing, and people feeling their hair being pulled, I met with the writer, went through the building, and tuned into the energy that was going on. I then had the writer get a hold of Sherri and had her do the same. It was actually fun, because she saw the exact same things that I had, felt the same things, and heard the same things. Which shouldn't be surprising since we were both in touch with truth and the energy that was present. After that, we did other work together. After a while, however, I chose to continue to do my work by touching and healing through my photography. Sherri will always touch, teach, and heal through her metaphysical works.

Sherri is the most popular intuitive consultant in northern

California, with eighteen years in private practice and more than thirty thousand readings to her credit.

She had a weekly television show, *Look Who's Talking*, from 1982 to 1986 and co-produced and hosted her own series for cable television, *The Psychic You*, in 1987, which is still being shown throughout northern California today.

In 1987, Sherri began teaching her own techniques for prenatal care and childbirth (*One Step Beyond—A Spiritual Approach to Childbirth*), in which the patient works with creative visualization, meditation, and prenatal massage. The leading OB/GYNs of her area welcome her assistance and have great respect for her work and how she affects the women with whom she comes in contact.

Sherri's most recent program is called *The Wise Woman Series,* in which she works with Celtic goddess mythology in combination with the Native American Medicine Woman's path to the approach to mid-life. The Wise Women Series are lectures, classes, and weekend workshops that allow women to connect to their ancient feminine heritage.

The realm in which Sherri works is wide. She gives private readings, conducts teaching workshops, and illuminates the path for bridging the gap from womanhood to the true meaning of the fruits of womanhood, menopause.

Sherri has always worked very hard for herself and for the community. She has raised thousands of dollars for the March of Dimes, AIDS research, the Arthritis Foundation, Children's Receiving Home, and the S.P.C.A. She also sits on the Board of Directors for the Mathews Foundation, a national organization that does funding for prostate cancer research and is affiliated with the U.C.D. Medical School at U.C. Davis, California.

Meditation Tape Available:
Through the Light—How to Meditate
On the Path—Color Meditation

Various workshops are available, and Sherri travels all over the country giving her lectures and is available for private consultation.

── Celeste ──
Visionary Artist

Celeste has years of impressive art training. Starting at age ten, for six years she took art classes at Carnegie Museum School in Pittsburgh, Pennsylvania. She received her master's degree at Penn State University, and she also studied at the University of London and in Holland. The list of her studies and her teachings goes on and on.

After years of study, she has developed her own visionary painting style. She plays some meditation music and gets herself centered, and her creativity simply flows. Spirit shows her visions and as if by magic the strokes of her brush seem to take over and create beautiful soul portraits. Celeste feels that her portraits help individuals to know themselves to be eternal beings of love, light, and power.

Often people get their soul portraits done by Celeste and come back to ask for spirit guide drawings or past life drawings. So it isn't always a one-time deal; people return.

On the phone, Celeste had arranged for me to mail her a portrait of myself so that she could do a soul portrait. So much of my work is done in black and white that, unthinking, I sent her a black and white photograph. I have dark red hair, but looking at the photograph one would think that my hair is dark brown. About a month later, I went to Sedona to see the results and hear the interpretation of the portrait.

I couldn't believe my eyes. And the first thing I did was cry. I thought that the drawing was so beautiful; everything seemed so familiar—and how in the world did she get my

hair color just right? She sat me down and told me that the portraits are unique for each person. We had a little meditation, where she tuned into my highest guidance at that moment. She explained that she then looks into the screen in her mind and instantaneously sees pictures. Many times, through channeling, spirits communicate with her by sharing her pictures, and as an artist she can draw these pictures. Through nonverbal colors and pictures, her meditation serves as a tool for getting immediately to your highest vibration through Spirit. As soon as Celeste began to talk to me, the tears poured down my cheeks. I didn't understand because I didn't feel sad. She said that I was feeling the love from my soul. None of this is about the ego, and each of us has a wonderful gift to give, but, as long as we're not in tune with our soul, we can't express it here. Celeste got into the energy too and then we both had tears. It was wonderful to feel this way. I could feel the energy from this piece of artwork—it was as though my soul really woke up.

After we meditated, Celeste began to interpret. The first thing that she got when she started the drawing was that I'm not from here; I'm from another place. There is a sadness because I'm very lonely here—I'm from a place where there is much more love, and I'm different from everyone around me. I know love among the stars, and there is a longing to go back where I belong. I'm in search of a unity that I simply can't find. I need to be with the other part of myself, which is called the twin soul or the mortal essence. A lot of expansive silver energy in the drawing is around my head, signifying that I'm not from here. Many spaceships. My energy has the technology and I am here to study and experience here for my group, and through me they get all of this understanding— what it's like to live in fear and separation, and to feel lonely. Where I'm from no one knows these feelings. As I go though my life here, I'm helping them to understand what it is like to live down here. Fortunately, there is a higher self that comes down and helps me through my problems.

The couples in the drawing represent a joy and a joy of life, an adventure of life here. She told me to trust the feelings that I have felt all of my life. As I listened to her, I knew that I've always felt these things, but no one had ever confirmed them for me.

Celeste connected with the total cosmic consciousness. In the picture there is a silver bird, which is a symbol of Spirit and my spirit wants to fly—to go back to the stars. The colors also present a story (although this black and white photograph doesn't allow my readers to see them). The colors are not earthly colors, but rather electric: silvers and blues along with magenta and purples. These colors help with sensitivity, the ability to tune in to other dimensions—spiritual, high-frequency, love energy that has been highly developed on other planets. On earth that's what this planet needs and that's what I am doing here. Earth will expand into this dimension.

Celeste's visionary soul portraits, paintings, prints, and greeting cards can be found in fine stores, galleries, offices, and homes throughout the country. She travels all over the country doing soul portraits, lecturing, and teaching classes.

Classes available:
Physical Ascension
Emotional Ascension
Mental Ascension
Spiritual Ascension

Books available:
Ascension Guidelines by Serapis Bey, channeled through Celeste & Jananda
The Phoenix: Symbol of Transformation by Apollo, channeled through Celeste
Tales of Jupiter by Jove, channeled through Celeste
Tales of the Planets

Soul Portraits
From a photo or in person. Revealing spirit guides, past life, and life purpose images and information.

Relationship Portraits
From a photo or in person, Celeste can show couples the karmic bands and mutual lessons that draw them together lifetime after lifetime. The result is a deeper understanding of one's essential goodness and contribution to the Divine Plan.

Sandra Dolan

Visionary Artist

It began well before Sandra was even born. Her grandfather and her great-grandfather were both artists in Russia, where they painted murals on church walls. With these genes it's no wonder that Sandra is also an artist.

Over the years Sandra has studied icon painting, fine arts, portraiture, and different ways for healing. She is a Reiki healer, and she incorporates all of her studying—art, metaphysics, and different forms of healing, both Eastern and Western—in her painting.

A major change came into her life when she began to study art with Hilda Charlton, a teacher of Ram Dass. Sandra traveled from Trenton to New York City once a week to study with her. After a pilgrimage with Hilda to sacred sites in Europe and India, Sandra's art changed drastically. Instead of doing traditional portraits, she began painting saints and angels. Sandra is well-known all over the world for soul portraits, but particularly for her paintings of angels.

Many things happen when Sandra does a soul portrait. Sandra focuses on the person's eyes, which are mirrors of the soul. She has the ability to reach into that person's aura and transcends an awakening through pastels onto the paper. In the drawing she lets Spirit guide her to the inner beauty of that person. Symbols and visions appear to her, and she allows Spirit to lead her to draw information which in turn allows the client goes through a true healing. Sometimes that healing is physical, emotional, mental, and spiritual, often a

healing of all those elements—and that is the reasoning for doing what she does, to heal and to see her clients claim their power of a balance of body, mind, and spirit.

Often, after Sandra draws soul portraits, the subjects want their guardian angels drawn. Clients often come back for more drawings, depending what is going on in their lives.

Sandra teaches workshops and draws both personal and group soul portraits in your home or in your center (or you can mail her a color photograph if you would like her to do your portrait long-distance).

—— Elaine Eagle Woman ——
Intuitive Consultant

Elaine Eagle Woman comes from a family of Apache medicine men and women. Shamanism and its sacred ceremony come naturally to her.

She remembers giving, in the fourth grade, readings to the other children using a crystal ball made of plastic. Her senses have always been wide open—seeing things, hearing things, feeling, and even smelling things. She has also always communicated with animals.

After the publication of Shirley MacLaine's book *Out on a Limb*, Elaine went to see Kevin Ryerson at a book store in Menlo Park. Kevin was channeling; all of a sudden, Elaine had an urge to speak, only it didn't feel like her voice that was trying to come through. She got up and left because she was afraid she would interrupt the event. She found herself trance channeling. She did this for several years, and decided that this was not the avenue that she wanted to travel.

When Elaine gives a reading, she goes into an altered state and starts the reading in layers, catching the surface and going into detail with different issues. Elaine also studies your handwriting—a skill that just "comes to her," with no formal training.

After engineering studies at Stanford University and working as an environmental chemist, she returned to school for a degree in psychology, which she uses in combination with her metaphysical and spiritual abilities.

She now resides in Sedona, Arizona, where she has her

practice. Elaine is a gifted healer utilizing body work, energy, channeling, and crystals therapeutically.

You can find Elaine in Tom Dongo's book *The Quest—The Mysteries of Sedona, Book III.*

CBS came to Sedona and had her on a segment of the show "48 Hours," called "Secrets of Sedona." She also appeared on New Zealand's "60 Minutes."

—— Patricia Hayes ——
Founder of Delphi
Artist
Healer
Medium

For some reason, I had a difficult time finding Patricia Hayes. (Once I found her, within a week I saw her on television twice, once on the sci-fi channel and another time on unsolved mysteries. When it rains, it pours.) My meeting got off to a bad start because, someone having told me that I could get from Virginia Beach to McCaysville, Georgia, in six hours, I was six hours late for our appointment. Patricia was very patient and kind with my very late arrival.

Patricia is an extraordinary artist. With pastels, she channels past lives and energy that is going on in this life time. A portion of her painting is on the cover of this book. Patricia interpreted the drawing for me and gave me a reading. She does a great deal of spirit drawings, or what she calls visionary art. She taps into your energy and spirit guides her through the drawing. In many cases people send her photographs for her to work from. At the institute she has an art gallery, The Oasis Art Gallery, which contains channeled art by Patricia Hayes and other artists; the art can be viewed and purchased. There is also a varied program of art workshops that are held throughout the year.

Patricia works at Delphi, a retreat that sits in the Blue Ridge Mountains in Georgia. It is located on a white-water river and includes 180 acres. Delphi is the home of:

The Patricia Hayes School of Inner Sense Development
The Arthur Ford International Academy of
  Mediumship
The Ro-Hun Institute
The Church of Wisdom
Etaph
Extension of Life Foundation

Some people come to Delphi for the actual healing, and others to become Ro-Hun therapists. Ro-Hun therapy is a form of healing developed by Patricia Hayes after more than twenty years of intensive study, research, and teaching. Through her dedication and experience, she has been able to perfect this holistic therapy where you move into the chakras and begin to move the energy. Energy is information; as the therapist begins to move the energy, the information begins to come to both the client and the therapist. Through the understanding of the cause, the energy can be released and at the same time the thought pattern can be both altered and spiritually understood. The therapy touches on every level. Patricia has trained therapists who now provide the therapy in about twenty-three countries. More information on this method of healing can be obtained from Patricia; it is also described in the book *Dancing Heart to Heart—The Story of Ro-Hun,* by Zolar.

Patricia worked with Arthur Ford for five years until he passed away. He was a world-renowned medium who channeled the book *Extension Of Life* through Patricia and her husband, Marshall. After Arthur's death, he came to her, and in three minutes he gave her the next twenty years of her life. Included in this information was a method of teaching mediumship that was fail proof. Patricia got together sixteen people, of all different ages and backgrounds, to do some experimenting, and sure enough, Patricia knew that she had to develop a training program for mediumship. This training is another of the opportunities available at Delphi.

There is also the Enoch Foundation, where private and group healing is available through the famous Mauricio Panisset, a Brazilian healer who uses the phenomenon of healing lights. Patricia has available a video that tells all about Delphi and shows its beautiful grounds; included on the video is an example of a healing done by Mauricio. I was astonished by what I saw. As he put his hands out and gave them somewhat of a shake, a flash of light actually burst from his hands, going over, around, and through the person who was receiving the healing.

There is also the Delphi-Brazil Project, which is a non-profit organization for an orphanage in Brazilia, Brazil, that provides a warm and loving home for forty homeless children. The program teaches leadership skills and awareness of self and others. The project's purpose is to return the children to their communities equipped to initiate change and help the 12 million homeless children in Brazil. (I might add that donations are very much appreciated!)

There is so much to share about Delphi, and I feel as though I have left so much out. Maybe you should find out for yourself. Patricia Hayes brings the most current spiritual and psychological leaders in the world to Delphi for their teachings. For information I recommend that you write for programs available.

Books Available:
The Gatekeeper
Extension of Life

Video:
The Delphi Experience

Classes:
Transformational Workshops
Ro-Hun
Mediumship
(The list is always changing.)

—— Jananda ——
Inter-Galactic Communicator
Healer
Teacher
Spiritual Counselor

Jananda is a published writer from Denmark. When he was in his thirties he had a serious back injury. After several major operations, all that modern medicine had to offer, and ten years of pain with no cure, he had an experience. A cosmic wake-up call which was the stimulus that caused him to look for other healing methods. In 1969 he had his first vision of his spiritual guide. His guide told Jananda that he had healing power in his hands, and asked him if he was ready to do his work. Jananda felt great elation, and this set him on his spiritual path.

Jananda ended up healing himself, and he gained great compassion for others who suffer. For the past twenty-five years, Jananda has dedicated his life to healing physical, emotional, and mental pain. However, Jananda does not do the healing; he assists you in healing yourself.

Jananda first looks into your auric field for the cause of your problems, whether it be improper nutrition, lack of self-love, or lack of self-forgiveness. Sometimes problems go deeper, such as those left over from many past lives. As soon as Jananda identifies the cause, he calls on the healing angels under archangel Raphael, calls on medical doctors on the hospital spaceships, or channels the Christ energy for healing through his own body to the patient. He uses different methods, including laying on of hands, reflexology, clearing the etheric body, and psychic surgery.

In 1979, during Jananda's meditation, a celestial being from the Cappella Star System appeared to him. In this meeting, Jananda was told about extraterrestrial origins. Since then, he has been working consciously with the Inter-Galactic Space Brotherhood. Jananda communicates with many different beings of thirty-three galaxies to bring peace to this part of the universe.

In 1988, after developing his intuition or intuitive abilities at a church in Copenhagen, he came to the United States as a guest speaker at a UFO conference in Seattle, Washington. He went home—to Denmark—and decided he needed to pack up and make the United States his home.

He met the beautiful Celeste. They married and settled in Sedona, Arizona, as so many intuitives do. Television critics from all over the world have come to Sedona to film programs which have included Jananda and Celeste.

Jananda holds open-house meditations every Saturday night in his home and also gives many lectures. His topics include healing, ascension, prophesies, changes, fear of ETs and UFOs, the last supper, and the Christ festival.

Ascension Guidelines include:
Physical Ascension
Emotional Ascension
Mental Ascension
Spiritual Ascension

Back From the Future includes:
Mystery Schools
Traveling Back Through Time to Past Lives
Spiritual and Intuitive Training

Tom Dongo's book *The Quest—The Mysteries of Sedona, Book III* includes information about Jananda.

The booklet "Ascension Guidelines" by Apollo, through Celeste and Jananda, can be purchased. Also available is a set of five tapes from Prescott Ascension classes.

—— Kathy Lawrance ——
Acupuncturist

Kathy Lawrance works with a traditional Chinese medical background in the ancient art of acupuncture. She received her master's degree in acupuncture and feels that education is very important and actually gives more creative allowance. Combining acupuncture, foot and body reflexology, and lymphology, she has a scope on all diseases.

My experience with Kathy was my first introduction to lymphatic massage, a therapy in which lymph glands are exercised to excrete toxins.

Kathy says that when she gets people on her table, they're put into alpha state, and, in addition to the healing that a patient receives, they quite often make major life decisions while lying there.

People often come to her with more than aches and pains or sickness. Most people who come to her are going through or about to go through a transformation. People are ready to step into the medicine path with a commitment, and she aids people with that change. Sometimes while she's working with someone the higher connection just clicks. At those times, she really enjoys her work; spirituality works under the guise of license.

Kathy's true love is the horse business. For twenty years she broke and exercised race horses. She received an injury while a mare was having a baby—she just about broke her back getting the fowl out because it was stuck. She became very ill and went to an orthopedic doctor, who wrote her a prescription for acupuncture. She was so helped, and so sold on acupuncture, that she decided to pursue it as her line of work.

Kathy's love for horses has also led her to working her medicine with horses. Yes, acupuncture for horses. Her practice in Sedona keeps her very busy, yet she also responds to calls out in the fields from ranchers needing assistance with their horses.

In addition to her practice, Kathy makes and sells Dream Pillows. She gave me one of her pillows; however, she told me to sleep with it only if I was ready to face my fears, my life, and things that I need to know. I carefully packed it and drove it home to Virginia with me. I was terribly curious about the pillow and its scent of different herbs and roots that it carried. I broke it out and placed it carefully under my pillow, dead center under my head, not knowing that I should have eased it there. I woke up in the middle of the night, sat up, and threw the pillow across the room. It was a bit much for me to handle at one time. I tucked it away for awhile, pulled it out again, and ever so gradually worked it to my pillow. I started off by placing it under my bed, and worked with it slowly. The amazing thing was that, in my dream time I would actually look at my life and different situations, and in that state be able to solve my problems. On occasions, I sleep with it when I feel I need a little insight.

Services
Acupuncture, Reflexology, and Lymphology
Horse Care
Dream Pillows
Spirit Guidance

Seminars
Spirit Awakening
Spirit Ceremonies
Meditation Group

William Lawrance (Wounded Eagle)
Shamanic Medicine Man
Artist

When I met Will Lawrance (Wounded Eagle), he took me around his grounds, showed me his sweat lodge, and took me into his tepee. It was huge and I was awestruck and filled with curiosity. Patiently he explained how he uses gourds, feathers, steer skulls, sticks, and pipes. He explained to me about the chanting and musical vibrations, and how the medicine man does what he does. To do something special for me, to give me a taste of what he does, Wounded Eagle had me lie down on the floor, which was covered with animal skins. He used an aborigines' instrument that he had made, something of a horn called a didgery-doo. As I lay there, he blew this instrument over the top of me, back and forth. I closed my eyes. It was incredibly strong, and before I knew it, I was floating at the top of the tepee looking down at myself. The tepee filled with fire; the flames danced to the top of the tepee, yet it was not hot. The fire went down, and at that point brilliant colors began to flash, as if in a light show. One would reasonably ask, did we smoke funny stuff in a peace pipe? But the answer is no, it was all very natural. As Wounded Eagle's music began to slow down, the colors became subdued and slowly faded out. I then became centered and slowly opened my eyes.

Wounded Eagle explained to me how he got his medicine

name. One day as he sat at his medicine wheel, smoking his pipe, the pipe broke. He then saw two visions. The first was of a wounded eagle. In the second vision, he saw an old medicine man and an elder. The elder walked up to an eagle with a bowl in his hands. The eagle spit blood into the bowl, and then the elder gave it to his friend, who wrote with the blood, on the ground inside the medicine circle, the name Wounded Eagle. Outside the tepee is a totem pole; on the pole is carved an eagle. When he walked past it the eagle's wing broke off, and that is how he got his name, Wounded Eagle.

When he works with people, he works with ancient medicines individualized for each person or group of people. As we come into this world we forget who we are and forget where we've been. Wounded Eagle helps people to tap into that state of remembering their purposes and shows people that they can have joy and happiness in their lives. As part of the healing ceremonies he goes through with people who come to him, he gets them to face their fears and weaknesses which can bring about sickness that can hold people back.

Wounded Eagle is also an artist. He makes beautiful medicine pots out of the Sedona red clay, along with medicine sticks, pipes, and Native American instruments.

As I was leaving, he gave me a beautiful medicine pot. Spirit had told him that I would be coming and he was to make this for me. He paints different designs on his pots, and on mine he had to paint an extraterrestrial on the side of it. It looked just like the one that came to me when I was meditating at the vortex at Boynton Canyon.

Available:
Sweat Lodge
Weddings
Medicine Wheel
Spirit Guidance
Ceremonies
Spirit Awakening Seminar
Spirit Ceremonies Seminar
Meditation Group Seminar

── Jeanie Loomis ──
Channel

Jeanie Loomis met Seth for the first time in 1975, during a clinical death. During an illness, one of her lungs collapsed and she was rushed to the hospital. As she was being wheeled into the emergency room, she had an out-of-body experience. Suddenly, there she was above her own body, looking down. She thought that it seemed as though her body had had an awfully short lifetime. Suddenly there was a massive presence, a light being. He said, "You haven't done what you were sent here to do; go back to your body." Part of her didn't want to because she felt so free.

He took her ahead in time and said, "Let me show you your mother." Jeanie saw that her mother was sad and tried to tell her not to grieve because she was with her. Her mother, however, couldn't hear her (because she didn't believe that she could hear). The energy or voice told Jeanie to go back to her body because she could service a link.

This energy enveloped her as she went into the emergency room. Jeanie had been clinically dead for about ten minutes, but the doctor insisted on bringing her back. He found a vein that was workable and he revived her. As she opened her eyes, she told him that she had died, but the doctor didn't want her to talk about it.

After she recuperated, Jeanie tried to go back to her daily life as a high school teacher and journalist. But her life was now different, and there was no going back. She kept hearing the voice that she heard while in the hospital. Jeanie would tell him to leave her alone, and he would remind her that she had work to do.

After some time she sought psychological counseling; after all, she was hearing voices and having hallucinations. She paid visits to several doctors, and one of them told her that she had experienced a valid psychic experience and should find a good parapsychologist.

She found a very good psychic, who told her that she needed someone with more expertise and referred her to another. This person encouraged her to meditate and to start working with astrology, which helped her to remember. The psychic suggested that they see if the voice would speak through her. Jeanie sat and asked for the voice to come through. In this way Jeanie began to channel Seth. He said that he was a collective energy and that Michael and Gabriel are part of this energy. The parapsychologist worked with her and after a year convinced Jeanie to open her own practice. At first she planned to limit this practice to the weekends. Soon, however, she gave up her teaching career to channel full-time.

In 1985 and 1986, she began doing channeling for the magazines *Body, Mind, & Spirit* and *Spirit Speaks.*

Clients from all over the world come to see her or have her do readings over the phone.

Jeanie also does rebirthing, helping people to move past their limiting thoughts about themselves and open up to new possibilities. For rebirthing, Jeanie has a person lie on a futon while she does full body harmony. She uses a hot tub for those who are ready to go under water. When Jeanie took rebirthing to a high school auditorium in Moscow, more than 400 people came to experience it. Some, hungry to know more about rebirthing, traveled a distance of 1200 miles.

Jeanie also conducts past life regressions. Using a brain wave synchronizer and hypnosis, Jeanie and Seth take people back.

Jeanie travels all over the world teaching, lecturing, and giving personal readings.

Lin David Martin

Trance Channel
Healer

Lin David Martin began his healing work in 1961. In 1971, after an eight-year study with an American Indian spirit teacher, he began his clairvoyant and trance practice. He worked for twelve years as a teacher and administrator with a Holistic Center in Phoenix.

Lin feels that this is a time of an awakening process termed *New Age.* A time of integrating many different elements, with the courage of the mystery schools of the past now available in the mystic tradition. The mysteries that were so hidden are now no longer hidden; they are available for those who are seeking.

During the last seventeen years, he has traveled all over the United States and Europe, offering his workshops in healing and intuition. He is finishing a book based on his experiences in altered states of consciousness and their relationship to healing.

When Lin goes into trance, he channels a wonderful and wise man, whom he has channeled for the past twenty years. His name is not given to us because he feels that is not important and that we should pay attention to the information that emerges instead of where this information comes from. The information that emerges gives us the power and clarity to make constructive changes and positive decisions in our lives.

As an insignificant but interesting side note, I found that

watching Lin go into trance and merge with this force was different than watching many others channel. Most channels take on different mannerism when they channel, but Lin's face seemed to take on characteristics of the energy that spoke through him; I had never seen anyone's face actually alter.

In the spring of 1993, Lin and his family Christine and Camilla moved from the bay area of San Francisco to Sedona, Arizona. Christine, his wife, is also a healer.

Lin offers four types of individual sessions. All of these sessions except healing ones are recorded for you. Phone sessions are also available, and there is truly no difference in a reading over the phone, because to Spirit, there is no distance.

Clairvoyant Reading

To do clairvoyant readings, Lin is in a state of clairaudience and clairsentience. He is in a light trance, therefore able to cover many different issues and a wide range of questions which means you can receive a large amount of information. This session is about 90 minutes long.

Healing

Healing sessions involve "laying on of hands," which is mainly a nonverbal experience, working with both the physical and non-physical bodies. Included is chakra balancing. A healing session is 30-60 minutes in length.

Extended Healing Session

In an extended healing session, Lin adds a verbal component to the laying on of hands. An assessment of the chakras is included. This session aids in understanding oneself and the chakras. An extended healing session is about 90 minutes long.

Trance Channeling

Here, Lin's personality is no longer present, giving you

direct access to Spirit. Lin describes the Teacher that he channels and offers the chance for people to experience themselves. Taped, the session is 60-90 minutes long.

Lin offers many classes, workshops, and retreats, including:
The Nature of Deep Trance
Healing—The Door to Ecstasy
Opening to Joy
Alignment with Purpose and Personal Prophesies

With Christine Bjorn Martin, he also offers a fairly new and intensive 14-day retreat through his school, called Opening Our Hearts To Nature. This retreat involves exploring Sedona and hiking the Grand Canyon. The major tools that are "played with" involve painting. Through painting and exercises at the Grand Canyon, Lin says, "you will find a way back home," to the child within. In Sedona, the high energy with guided meditation and healing processes will lead you to feel the connection of grounding and of nature, bringing about a time of empowerment of Body/Mind/Spirit.

Robin Miller

Musical Artist
Past Life Regressionist
Trance Channel

Robin had his first spiritual experience at age four. An angel came to his bedside, comforting him and telling him of his mission and his purpose in this incarnation. He has known all his life that he was put here to heal, to bring joy and love into people's lives, and to help others to learn to love themselves so that they too can unite and become one with the universe.

At age ten, he had an encounter with a UFO. He lived in Detroit, and one and a half miles from his house was a dirt race track. He, a friend, and his parents were all outside in the backyard having a barbecue when the sky lit up, and hovering over the race track was a spaceship. Everyone panicked, his friend got scared and ran home, and his parents ran into the house and started making phone calls to report it. The lines were all busy, which they assumed meant that everyone else who saw it was doing the same thing. While everyone was acting, Robin stood there in awe without any fear and felt very familiar with its presence. There was an energy that seemed to be communicating with him. When it first appeared, it simply came out of nowhere, and when it left, it shot straight up and was instantly gone, leaving as quickly as it arrived. Robin knows that he has been a part of another place in this universe.

When he was fifteen, he was introduced to yoga, and at sixteen initiated to Kriya Yoga.

For the past twenty-five years, Robin has been an accomplished songwriter, singer, and performer, channeling Jonothon. His music is absolutely magical and breathtaking.

I first met Robin in a little cafe in Sedona, where I stopped for breakfast. He was there playing his music, and my daughter and I were enchanted by the magic that he was making. As you listen to his music, you also *feel* it. You can feel it dancing in your heart, bringing you to your higher self, bringing all your elements to become one with one another. His truly inspiring music is excellent for meditation. His channeled music, a transformational blend of pianos and synthesizers, has been met with critical acclaim.

In addition to channeling music, Robin is also a trance channel and past life regressionist. He conducts individual and group workshops to help people discover their past lives. Through the regression, you will recognize the origins of your fears and release their destructive hold upon you, witness your birth and death within several life experiences, and connect with your spirit guide to feel the unconditional love of your higher self.

A series of books are being written by Robin, channeled from his Master Teacher, Jonothon of the Seventh Ray, Speaker of the Council of the Brotherhood of Light.

You can also read the writings of Jonothon through Robin every month in the *Sedona Journal of Emergence.*

Tapes and CDs available:
Paradise View
Magical Spheres
Celestial Bridge
From My Heart

Books available:
Talks with Jonothon: Book I
The Path of Love: Book II
(There will be three more books in this series.)

Robert Monroe

Founder of The Monroe Institute
The Ultimate Explorer

Bob Monroe's story begins in 1958. He and his wife Nancy were living in Westchester County; they owned several radio stations and other businesses and had offices on Madison Avenue in New York. He was very successful, but an event came over him that would change him for the rest of his life.

For no apparent reason, he began to float out of his body. The phenomenon continued to happen and made him very curious. He thought that maybe he was ill, or dying, or who knows. He spoke to psychiatrists and psychologists about the experiences, but he was assured that there was nothing wrong with him.

He called these trips OBEs, out-of-body experiences. He set up an office to do research and gather more information about this strange happening. He wanted to learn more about it, how to control it, and how to develop it. He began doing experiments with it, using friends for his testing. Later this research division became known as The Monroe Institute.

The best way to know about Robert Monroe and The Monroe Institute is to read his books. He writes about his adventures, his experiences, and many of the studies and experiments that take place at the Institute. The books also give you idea of what a week at The Monroe Institute can do for you. Through his courses, you can shape your life, change your life, let go of fears, learn to accept that you can cross any boundaries that you may have set for yourself, and learn how to travel in time and space.

There are two divisions of the Institute. The Educational Division involves classes and seminars and uses and distributes audio tapes and other materials that apply to the methods that have been developed. The Research Division continues the study of the human consciousness development of methods and techniques for further use.

The Monroe Institute offers several major applications and programs:

Gateway

Gateway consists of exercises that are dedicated to the development and understanding of the total self; finding what we are and what we do when we sleep. Seminars are held, and there are audio tapes for an in-home exercise series. Through this program we learn to move from one level of consciousness to another and to examine these different levels and be able to recreate these different states of consciousness at will.

Guidelines

In the Guideline program, participants practice to make tape recordings of their experiences as they happen. You are also shown how to contact your Inner Self-Helper and how to communicate with other intelligences. The ability to receive information about the past, present, and the future is there.

Lifeline Program

The Lifeline Program takes the consciousness into areas beyond physical death. One of the experiences here is finding those that have gone to the other side but are trapped between life and death—in actuality, lost. These are often people that have died suddenly, in an accident, for example, or may have unfinished business which holds them back. In this program, we find these souls, take them where they can rest, and allow them to find their way home.

Another program is called Hemi-Sync 2000. Hemi-Sync is the name given to the technology which, through sound patterns, alters brain waves so that the two hemispheres of the brain work together. There are numerous tapes available using this technology, and outcomes from the use of them are remarkable—even astounding—in many cases.

Thousands of people from all over the world have visited The Monroe Institute, gathering healing, self-discovery, and the exploration of states of consciousness.

Books available:
Journeys Out of the Body
Far Journeys
Ultimate Journey

A list of the dozens of tapes available can be obtained from The Monroe Institute.

—— Kathy Oddenino ——
Registered Nurse/Healer

You can find Kathy Oddenino in Annapolis, Maryland. She is a retired nurse and has been in the medical field for more than forty years.

Her experience as a registered nurse includes work with Georgetown University Medical School, The National Institutes of Health, The Naval Medical Research Institute, The Uniformed Service University of Health Sciences, and many major medical centers. Now she lectures and conducts seminars all over the country. She also gives personal and energy readings, offers retreats, and has appeared on various radio and television talk shows discussing nutrition as based on her spiritual beliefs. She is also the author of books and 150 audio tapes available for purchase.

Kathy works with the physical things that support the body, including nutrition, exercise, and life style. She deals with smoking, drinking, and other addictions or dependencies and with one's attitude—healing the mind as well as the body and the spirit.

Her work is based on the knowledge that you need to accept your personal responsibility for living; when you do, you have got it made, and you can do whatever you want to do. The thought that you cannot do something, for whatever reason, is just an excuse. You—we all—have the ability to access, to use all three parts of your mind. When you can do this, you will no longer have disease. Kathy insists that you look in the mirror, at your reflection, and see the beauty of who you are. Know that you can change!

Kathy helps you support your immune system and cellular structure by getting the right nutrition. She urges you to look at what you eat, drink fresh water, breathe fresh air, do the things that will support your immune system, and remember that medicine knocks out your immune system. She looks for new ways to allow you to heal yourself by paying attention to your relationship to nature.

I asked Kathy what she would do with me if I came to her for counseling. She asked me what is wrong with me in a physical sense, and I told her of a disease I have in my spine which causes severe neck and back pain. She told me that my body needs to heal itself and told me what to eat and what not to eat. (Of course, all of the things that I shouldn't eat, that are affecting my condition, I eat plenty of.) I followed her advice to the letter, and, just six weeks later, the pain was gone. All I did was change my diet. After a year, the disease doesn't even exist in my body. Who would have thought that changing your diet could make a disease completely disappear? (Between Kathy Oddenino and all of the other hands that have been on me in the course of writing this book, I should be living two lifetimes in this one little body!)

Books available
The Joy of Health
Bridges of Consciousness
Sharing: Self-Discovery in Relationships
Love, Truth and Perception
Unveiling the Mystery of Disease

Kathy offers workshops and retreats and can provide information about them.

—— Rinatta Paries ——
Astrologer
Numerologist
Bach Flower Therapy Practitioner

Rinatta is from Russia and lives in San Diego. I gave her all of my birth information and we met the following day on the beach, where she interpreted my astrological chart. She emphasizes in her work spiritual issues that you are dealing with on a karmic level. In other words, she feels that you have come into this lifetime with a set of issues and you will always have difficulty dealing with them until you have addressed them. Through the astrological chart, Rinatta can see these issues and work with you to learn how to deal with them.

There are many avenues that Rinatta uses with her clients. She uses acupuncture, herbology, and medical astrology to pinpoint physical and emotional difficulties in her patients. She has also studied Reiki and, depending on the needs of the person, utilizes whatever she feels a patient may need. Sometimes she uses Reiki along with acupuncture. When she speaks with her clients, she works with their energy as well, to attune their energy so that they can hear what she is saying, so that they can make the shifts and changes in their lives necessary to attain harmony and spirituality. Once the needles are in place during an acupuncture session, she does Reiki, as an enhancement to the acupuncture. The bach flower remedies are used primarily to balance out the emotional-spiritual body, so that she can receive the answers to particular

questions and thereby diagnose and prescribe bach remedies and put together individual formulas. These methods correspond with numerology. According to Rinatta, bach flower remedies have their own numerological correspondence in value in working with clients, karma, and their issues that they are dealing with in their lives.

A great deal of Rinatta's counseling is marital and family counseling.

Classes:
Astrology, Basic and Advanced
Finding Your Soul Mate (This class is designed to address emotional and spiritual issues underlying repeated dysfunctional patterns in relationships. After the class, most people have found healthy relationships. Included are rituals, such as ceremonial candle burning. Spiritual issues are covered as well as emotional issues.)

Rinatta also offers an Astrological Dating Service.

—— Foster Perry ——
Shaman/Medicine Man

It is an ancient Inca tradition that if you go to the top of a mountain during a lightning storm and tempt the lightning to hit you to prove that you want to be a shaman, and you truly have that ability, you will get hit. This is exactly what Foster Perry did, and he did get hit by lightning. He experienced a Kundalini, changing his life. For a month he packed this electricity around with him, healing everyone that he touched. He began to see and speak to Spirit and remembered his past lives. His story is well told in his book *When Lightning Strikes a Hummingbird.* Foster is based in Santa Fe and in Brazil.

There are four aspects to his healings and readings. For a personal consultation, he will tell you all about yourself from the letters in your name. This process usually takes about three hours. It's very deep, and sometimes he goes through your body to find out what is going on with you physically or—more significant to him—emotionally. He looks in your skin and remembers events in your life and helps you to release whatever attachments you have to the past or see the past in a new light.

Hands-on healing and physical adjustments are sometimes done. He also does rebirthings, but differently from traditional rebirthings. He has you do a circular form of breathing, in which the in-breath and the out-breath are one breath, very much like hyperventilating; while you do so, he presses on the body doing deep massage, very similar to rolfing. During

81

the screaming and yelling, he brings back things from your childhood, past life or birth trauma. Finally, he has you birth yourself, actually going through the process of pushing the child out. Afterwards he mummifies you and wraps you in blankets and towels. You then go through a death, singing death chants with your body in preparation. Foster then explains the Egyptian form of death; he takes off the garments, and you are then reborn.

A regression, taking three to six hours, is also done. Foster takes you, through a meditation, through your body and out. He teaches the journey, and you see all of the lives on earth and other dimensions. The goal is to find your soul and then you can find your eternal self. Through the journey you go to the beginning and see your creator.

People visit Foster and stay anywhere from a week to a month. He teaches how to work with local herbs and local weeds to make remedies to heal your body. He teaches the woman wise medicines (which is mostly woman's domain, but Foster likes doing it).

He introduces you to the four sacred mountains around Santa Fe and you go to the top and do a ceremony there. You meet the four elements and your power animal. You do a water ritual in which you may go to the ocean or river and have a vision or a physical experience. From the air may come to you an eagle or a hawk, a raven, or a crow. He takes you on a vision quest where you may meet your earth animal, either physically or in a vision. Your power animal may be a fire animal, in which case you do a fire ceremony and you dance around the fire. The rituals introduce you to earth, serving as tools for connecting to God through creation.

Foster leads you on a journey where you look at your shadow, spending maybe a week looking at the darkness in your life and doing shadowy things, all the things that you think are taboo for you. You experience all your sexual taboos and programming from this culture, learning to put down nothing in creation.

Foster sees his whole body. He is very interested in pain, loss, and grief, and he has worked in hospices for years, helping people in transition, such as patients of AIDS, cancer, and old age, to die. With a strong interest in death, which is a shaman's domain, he releases the fear of death, breathing in everyone's pain and breathing out joy, love, and healing, and taking on patients' pain to change it, like transportation.

Foster does many workshops. They are all spontaneous, with nothing prepared. Participants dance, bringing fire into their bodies through dancing, sing, mimic one another, and do everything one would do in a tribe, including wrestling. These activities bring about the tribal mind. You participate in poetry readings, and you interact with one another and let out your secrets, things that you've never wanted anyone to know. Foster goes through the body of everyone who comes to the workshop. Songs are sung to people.

Foster also offers tours. He and another shaman accompany a 50-person tour to Peru; also available are tours to the Amazon and to six countries in Europe. He offers a retreat in Bali, with Bali healers. Foster's goal is for the people on the tour to become a part of the culture they visit.

He has a nonprofit organization called AYMARA, for environmental issues and for spiritual study for indigenous people. He lives with a group in Brazil called Xavantes and they're building a place for him there. He worked to become a warrior initiate.

Foster learns about other cultures and distant places so that he can integrate that knowledge into his own work. Cultures are now blending and he goes every year to the same places and helps the people. Not only does Foster travel all over the world, but he also travels all over this country doing his workshops.

I met with Foster when he was doing a workshop at the Mercy Center, in Madison, Connecticut. In response to my request for a piece of him so that I could see how he works, he read me some poetry and then he sang to me. His songs are very long—sometimes he sings for an entire day. The chant he sang for me was beautiful. As he sang, I closed my eyes and went with him. We went on a beautiful journey. I was a mermaid dancing in the ocean to his music that he sang. I also met with my animal spirit and a scorpion. It truly was incredible. I taped the song, and every time I listen, I get something new out of it.

Books:
When Lightning Strikes a Hummingbird
Violet Forest—Journey to the Amazon

Album:
We Dyed the Wheatfields Gold (Brazilian hip-hop meditations)

Film:
Road Scholar (MGM)

Foster Perry also has a series of videos.

—— Sally Perry ——
(Spirit Medicine)
Medicine Woman

Virginia Beach is graced with the presence of part-Cherokee medicine woman Sally Perry, whose Indian name is Spirit Medicine. She began this journey as a medicine woman in 1977.

Sally offers many workshops. In one, everyone makes an honoring stick, covering it with crystals, feathers, and other materials. This is a transformational and transitional workshop. Covering a stick represents a part of you sometimes discarded by transforming and transmuting into new life—a part of you that has died. By covering the form of the stick you are honoring it—that energy comes back to you as a form of healing.

Sally also offers vision quests for four to twelve people. During a vision quest, no food or water is allowed. Recognizing that only you can heal *you*, this quest helps you to identify your own quest and to get in touch with your own spirit, including your own healing. Sally feels that we need to all start healing ourselves so that we can be examples for those around us to learn to heal themselves. She demonstrates the strength of the medicine man or woman—the ability to show you how to work on your mental, emotional, physical, and spiritual selves. How to honor your soul and everything around you.

Sally, or Spirit Medicine, is an ordained minister and interned for fourteen years with the world-famous Native

American shaman Beautiful Painted Arrow, in Colorado. From him she experienced many facets of the shaman way of life and feels that she was put here to work as a Rainbow Bridge to teach others, and to help others learn to heal their souls.

Spirit Medicine at this time has completed eleven World Peace Dances and performed countless sweat lodges, vision quests, and medicine wheels.

Since 1986, for two to three months out of the year Sally travels and assists the Reverend Alex Orbito, the world-famous healer from the Philippines to whom Shirley MacLaine has referred in her writings.

Sally spends a great deal of the time traveling all over the world teaching the medicine way. She also offers private consultations as a clairvoyant and works with her ancient self/spirit medicine, in workshops and seminars.

When I sat with her, she held my hand and began talking about things going on in my life and specific things that will be coming up. She invited me to be her guest at a sweat lodge that she was holding the following Sunday. Having never been to a sweat before, I didn't know what to expect, but I was very excited.

Before entering the sweat lodge, the women changed into skirts and tops and the men wore shorts. We made prayer bundles; everyone made ten each. Prayers are offered honoring the East, South, West, and North, Father Sky, Mother Earth, and the Heart, which is our center. After we made the prayer bundles, we put them all together and we formed a circle around the bundle, chanting and performing a healing circle. As we sat on the floor, all facing the left, we worked on each other's back, with the left hand on the shoulder and the right hand over the person's heart. We channeled healing energy into that person, and sent that energy around the circle. A very handsome young man sat in front of me by the name of Curt, and there was a man behind me. I didn't really pay too much attention to the energy that the man was sending me from behind; I was more concerned about this man in front of me because he was in real need of healing. I could feel his aching heart, his soul and his body. His body was like a vacuum, sucking the energy from my fingertips. He weakened and sank into my arms. I could feel the sadness in his heart.

After this healing, we lined up and stepped outside to head over to the sweat lodge. Snow was on the ground, it was about ten degrees below zero, it was evening, and here I was wearing these little sandals and a light-weight skirt. I just about froze as I slipped off my sandals before entering the lodge, feeling the snow under, over, and through my toes. Sally led the sweat; through prayer she helped us all to face our own selves, and helped us to see and experience the true meaning of body/mind/spirit well-being.

The sweat was a unique experience. I was sweating in places I didn't know I had. It felt absolutely wonderful. I could see myself letting go of negative energy. When I entered, my sinuses were aching, which also made my teeth ache, but once I got in there and opened myself up, all of the discomfort went away. But the spiritual experience was the most meaningful, of course. When I was in there, when we addressed the Grandmothers, Grandfathers, and Spirits of all the directions, I saw the lodge open up and at the top were these energies, with all their arms extended, holding a huge crystal.

The following month I did another sweat with Sally. This time the lodge filled with doves, and my heart went out and danced throughout the lodge. My next sweat was a little different. The lodge filled with baby deer; they all, one at a time, came to me, stepped in and became a part of me. The deer represented unconditional love. Each time I enter the sweat lodge, wonderful experiences surround me.

Even better, however, was the twenty-four-hour vision quest that I experienced. If you really need some medicine, you'll receive whatever it is that you might need during this ceremony. You'll feel the earth move under your feet.

I try to go to one of Sally's sweat lodges or visit her medicine wheel once a month. I find I want to do Native American ceremonies; they keep me grounded, remind me to not be judgmental, and help me to hold the light.

Sally is a true healer and represents the Mother of this Earth.

Sally Perry's work is presented in:
Private Healing Consultations
Vision Quests
Story Telling
Workshops and Seminars
Medicine Wheel & Sweat Lodge
Private Ceremonies—Weddings and Land Blessings

—— Mary Reagan ——
Trans-Personal Astrologer

An astrologer and spiritual counselor, Mary lives in the mountains of Sedona. She is also a master Reiki healer.

Mary likes to touch on karma when she does your chart. She says that by dealing with karma, both positive and negative, you find it easier to get on with your life. When she does a chart, she interprets it and, through channeling, is able to add a great deal of information that doesn't show up in the chart.

There are other tools that Mary uses for reading. She calls them her magician tools: tarot, numerology, Kabala.

She also writes monthly horoscopes for publications, including *Sedona Journal of Emergence.*

Mary offers workshops, lectures, and teaching of all levels of astrology. She also offers readings, which are 60-90 minutes and are taped for your convenience.

Horoscopes that are available:
Natal (Birth)
Progression (Yearly Update)
Synastry (Two Charts Compared)
Return (Exact Times of All Planetary Conjunctions)
Transits (Location of the Planets at any Given Time)

Pat Rodegast
Channel

Pat Rodegast is famous for the channeling of Emmanuel. Emmanuel has been with her for twenty years, guiding her and others with love, compassion, and truth. About what she experiences when she channels, Pat said, "I am aware of what Emmanuel says. I'm not unconscious, I'm not warm, I'm just this far back, just a tiny bit." Years ago when she first started, it truly was a struggle: she wanted to know what's me—what isn't me—what's truth—what isn't truth. Emmanuel taught her that we have come to bring spirit and humor together, so there is no getting away—no escaping; her responsibility as a human being was to be as clear as she could. In the beginning she said it was awful because she wanted to float on the ceiling. But that's not exactly how it happened.

As Pat told me these things, she stopped our conversation and told me that Emmanuel had something he wanted to tell me. As she sat there, she closed her eyes and almost instantaneously Emmanuel was with us. His words were eloquently spoken and I could see a beautiful light surrounding Pat as she spoke his words. After he talked to me, he asked if I had any questions. I had none because he had told me everything that I needed to know.

I asked Pat, "Who is Emmanuel?"

She replied, "Who is Emmanuel? He is a being of light—he has been human, and no thank you—he doesn't want to be human again. He is a bridge between perfect love and us. He is also a teacher."

What she loved about him from the beginning was that he would always hand back decisions to seekers. He never says do this, do that; he says you might look at this and maybe the pain is from that. But he's always been honoring of people; otherwise, Pat says, she couldn't have done it.

"What else?" I asked.

She said, "I guess he's an angel."

Ten years ago, Emmanuel told her to stop giving personal consultations. She travels all over the world giving workshops, lecturing, and channeling Emmanuel for large groups. She also writes. Her books are truly inspiring; the writings are beautiful. *Emmanuel's Book I* is a book of questions and answers. The wide range of topics include God, Light and Christ, love, religion, Spirit, evil and pain, fear, joy, karma, reincarnation, illness and healing, death, marriage and divorce, sexuality, and other planets. The book includes a section of exercises dealing with, among other things, issues of loving yourself, dealing with fear, and discovering yourself.

The books by Pat and Emmanuel are beautiful and are filled with much love and wisdom. I have learned so much from them, and, by using what I have read, I have a better understanding of many facets of my life.

Workshops are available.

Books:
Emmanuel's Book I: A Manual for Living Comfortably in the Cosmos
Emmanuel's Book II: The Choice for Love
What's an Angel Doing Here?

—— Kevin Ryerson ——
Author
Educator
Trance Channel

Kevin Ryerson—where do I begin? He's the most famous trance-channel in the world today. I first met him in 1986, when I photographed him during a lecture in Sacramento. Five years later, I requested a reading from him, and he channeled his partner Obediah for me. I have had many readings and from many people, but I'll tell you, the reading that Kevin gave me was the most valuable dollar I ever spent. Obediah gave me wonderful insight and guidance. He had a sense of humor and acted at one point as though he were my grandfather (an attitude, I might add, that I needed). I asked him about this book; he confirmed that it was a great idea and gave me some insight on it. Interestingly, in my reading I was told that I would approach a publisher for the book and it would be rejected, but that the second publisher would grab it right up. Of course, I didn't believe it—I had never written a book before and figured I would go through at least thirty publishers before I would find someone. I approached my second publisher (I had a list of publishers a mile long, thinking that I would need a long list) and found that Obediah knew exactly what he was talking about because it was that publisher who took me on. I was shocked—and when I realized that I actually had a publisher, then I had to get the book done! I pulled out the tape that Kevin had made for me from the reading to see what else was in store for me. I have all kinds of changes and goodies to look forward

to, but I'll take one step at a time.

Kevin is an author, a lecturer, an award-winning film consultant, and an expert intuitive, and he is well-known in the field of parapsychology. Kevin authored the book *Spirit Communication: The Soul's Path*, a wonderful book on channeling, and has contributed to several books.

Kevin Ryerson is the man who Shirley MacLaine quotes in *Out On A Limb*, and he is featured in the movie with the same name, playing his own part. He is also an award-winning film consultant who worked on Steven Speilberg's *Poltergeist II.*

Kevin travels all over the world giving seminars and retreats, and follows up with private sessions. As most of the people in his book, he also gives readings long-distance; he does not need you there in the physical.

Kevin does business as Kevin Ryerson and Company, the "company" being John, Tom MacPhearson, and Obediah. John inhabits an ancient Essene community, where his colleagues authored the Dead Sea Scrolls. To me he seems so serious all the time, whereas Tom MacPhearson, who lived 400 years ago in Elizabethan England, has quite the sense of humor along with his wonderful accent. Obediah is an herbalist who lived on Haiti circa 1843. Together the three of them consult and advise. Recently Kevin Ryerson and Company traveled to Egypt and contributed to the interpretation of hieroglyphics and mythology by channeling in the presence of acknowledged authorities.

Kevin offers many different seminars and workshops. Times, places, and topics vary; you can find out what may be in your area and get information about his tele-readings (readings via telephone) by getting on his mailing list.

Books:
Mysteries of the Unknown, Time-Life Book Series
Spirit Communication: The Soul's Path
Kevin Ryerson contributed to the following books:
Psychoimmunity—Key to the Healing Process

Spiritual Nutrition
Channeling: The Intuitive Connection

Kevin's intuitive abilities are mentioned in Shirley MacLaine's best-selling books *Out on a Limb, Dancing in the Light,* and *It's All in the Playing.*

Television Appearances:
"The Oprah Winfrey Show"
"Good Morning America"
CNN's "Crossfire"
"The Joan Rivers Show"
(And the list goes on and on!)

—— Mother Sarita ——
Healer/Psychic Surgeon

Hermana Sarita was born in Guadalajara in 1912. She married at the tender age of fourteen and had the first of her thirteen children at age fifteen. She worked hard all of her life to support this large family.

In the early '60s she became ill. She had chest pains and a heart murmur, and she was told by doctors that she had gallstones and would die if she didn't have an operation. Her sons balked at her being operated on, but doctors in Tijuana and San Diego gave her the same diagnosis. Sarita returned to Tijuana to see her elderly mother, who urged her to visit a temple of spiritual healing. She did not believe in such things, but finally, to appease her mother, she went to the temple to meet a psychic healer named Petro Castro. Petro convinced her to undergo psychic surgery.

During the surgery Sarita thought that she was going through a physical operation. She watched them remove fourteen stones and heard them hit the dish as she counted them one by one. Informed that the operation had been completely spiritual, Sarita was converted to a believer.

After her surgery, Sarita began a three-year apprenticeship with Petro. Her spirituality grew and she learned to perform psychic cures.

When I went to meet with Sarita, I was met at the door by her grandson, who interprets for her because she speaks no English. He demonstrated an obvious respect for his grandmother and took very good care of her. When Mother

Sarita entered the room, I could hardly believe my eyes. Knowing her age, I had expected a short, wrinkled old woman. I was right about her height—she was short—but her looks belied her age. She had black hair and smooth skin, and she was dressed in sequins. She had a certain youth about her, and when she smiled her eyes sparkled.

Her grandson put in the VCR a video of one of her surgeries that was taped by a camera crew for a television show. It started with a woman pulling up her blouse so that we could clearly see her stomach, which had a large lump, a tumor. The tape showed the surgery and then showed a close-up of her stomach after the surgery, and the tumor was no longer there.

Mother Sarita does her surgery in her immaculate home, where she has her *Temple de Medio Die* (Temple of God's Medicine). She is also a spiritual counselor at *Casa Familiar* (Family House), which is a community social service agency in San Ysidro, along the border of Mexico.

All of her abilities are channeled through her spiritual teacher known as Gray Eagle's Foot Red Skin. She also communicates with some extraterrestrials, who have given her the plans for a pyramid healing center that she and her organization are to build.

Classes available:
Be Your Own Healer
Awake the Full Potential of Your Mind
Read Auras

Lecture Topics and Demonstrations:
Spiritual Operations and Healings
Clairvoyance
Slide Presentation on Spiritual Healing
Audience Participation Solicited for Demonstration

Healing Services:
Psychic Healings
Personal Psychic Readings

—— Gordon-Michael Scallion ——
Futurist

Gordon-Michael Scallion lives in a small town in New Hampshire, which makes a trip to see him a beautiful drive. However, reliable weather predictions are helpful—which is exactly what Gordon does: he predicts earth changes. When I called him to let him know the dates that I would be in New England and that I wanted to include him in the book, he informed me that he had predicted a treacherous storm to hit New England that would knock their socks off. He had predicted the storm several months before and was scheduled to leave the day before the storm was to hit for a nice vacation in Florida. According to Gordon, the day I would arrive in Rhode Island would be his last day there, and the following morning he would be leaving to finer weather. I interviewed him as planned, and the next morning Gordon was on his plane to sunny Florida, I was on the road to Connecticut, and Gordon's prediction had turned out to be most accurate. I'm sure everyone remembers that storm in January of '94, which seemed to go on forever. I found it interesting that this man could be so accurate with his timing of the storm; three months prior, he had his plane tickets for the day before the storm hit!

Gordon's gift of predictions didn't seem to be a gift at the very beginning. It all started in 1979 with an illness which caused him to lose his voice. Within twenty-four hours, a change came over him. He started hearing voices and seeing things. The phenomenon became stronger and stronger, and he actually thought that just maybe he had gone over the edge a bit. His voice did return, but the loss of it for just a short while brought on other senses which remained, and his life would never be the same. People started coming to him for spiritual guidance and healing. It became overwhelming, and he began to have nightmares, twenty-eight days of nightmares. After the twenty-eighth day, he began writing down his dreams. He wrote them in a newsletter-type form and mailed them out to a hundred people that he knew. Letters started pouring in from people who wanted to subscribe to this new newsletter. At that point he stopped giving private counseling and began his publication *The Earth Changes Report.*

This newsletter is read in thirty-eight countries and all states. The predictions that he makes are of earth changes—things that happen to the planet such as earthquakes, floods, economic trends, conflicts in the world, diseases, miracles, and manifestations. He follows up in his newsletter, reporting on the accuracy of each prediction after the fact. He has also made available his *Future Map of the United States: 1998-2001*, which presents his vision of what the country will look like, with new coastlines, following the earth changes that he predicts will occur. Additionally, Gordon has available videos and tapes taken from seminars or from special interviews.

Gordon travels to areas for presentations, if he has seen changes in those areas.

Sandi Staylor

The Village Psychic

Sandi has studied comparative religion since the age of fourteen, when she lived in a Jewish temple for two years. She has a great deal of knowledge about religion, most of which is an inner knowledge, brought forward from a past life that she lived in Egypt.

She has been giving readings for the past thirty-eight years. In 1973, she was invited to become a charter member of the American Society of Occult Sciences, founded by Hans Holzer. She is also a member of the A.R.E. in Virginia Beach.

Sandi believes that we are busy creating our tomorrows today; consequently our energy gives us an idea of the path that we're on and what is coming up on that path. The future isn't carved in stone, because we have the ability to change that energy. That is the reason for getting a reading: if we are creating right now our tomorrow, we have the ability to change what we see that we're creating—change the outcome.

When you come to Sandi for a reading, she first thoroughly explains her process. Then she begins to read a little bit of your palm and from that she taps into your energy force that is in the center of your palm, one of the energy vortices of the body. When Sandi was a young girl, she befriended a gypsy woman and learned as much from her about palmistry as she possibly could. She says the way that she reads the palms may not be what you may find in the books, but her method works for her.

Sandi is also a hands-on healer. While I was in her metaphysi-

cal institute, I met a woman who had been hospitalized for emphysema and who had then experienced a series of healing sessions with Sandi. She had no signs that I could see of any illness. She was bearing a gift for Sandi, in gratitude. Sandi's real goal, more than channeling healings, is to teach people how to heal themselves, how to channel the energy for healing, to help themselves and to be able to help those with whom you come in contact.

Sandi travels with her workshops and lectures, and gives clairvoyant readings.

Lectures and Workshops:
Psychic Development
Ancient Spirit Philosophy
Lesser and Greater Mysteries of Ancient Egypt
Meditations
Spiritual Healing/Spiritual Counseling

—— Robert Van de Castle, Ph.D. ——
Dream Expert
Consultant

Dr. Robert Van de Castle has worked extensively for more than thirty years with dreams. He was a professor at the University of Virginia for twenty-five years, researching and teaching every conceivable aspect of dreams.

He is the author of the recently-published book *Our Dreaming Mind.* This book covers every aspect of dreams, including how dreams today differ from dreams years ago, the scientific side of dreaming, and the creative aspects of the dream. His book discusses both the Jungian and the Freudian theories, as well as Native American beliefs. Native Americans often used ceremonies with and for dreams, and Dr. Van de Castle uses these same ceremonies to bring on dreams for guidance and self-healing.

During Dr. Van de Castle's early years at the University of Virginia, he was the director of the sleep and dream laboratory. He found that he was always more interested in the dream side of what was going on. He later became the director of clinical psychology, and it was then possible to work with dreams individually and with groups and collective dreams in Panama and other areas in Central America. His book includes a compilation of his thirty years of experience in working with dreams and his travels to distant places to do so.

One of the areas with which the doctor works is dream sharing. A target, or dreamer, dreams, and others, called dream helpers, tune into the target's dreams as they sleep. When everyone awakens the next morning, the dreams are shared; each dream helper's dream will be different, but all will relate to the target's dream. When all are pulled together, like a puzzle, they will all fit, thereby helping the target to understand himself or herself. The dream helpers are actually telepathically getting into the target's dream. Through the study of your dreams a tremendous amount of healing can be done whether it be through spontaneous or illusive dreams or through a dream-helper ceremony.

Dr. Van de Castle shared many of his adventures and his Native American ceremonies with me. He travels all over the country to do dream ceremonies for groups, and he has a private dream consultation business.

He is the most knowledgeable dream expert in the world, and he has been on numerous talk shows and specials—including shows on the Discovery Channel, Barbara Walters' specials, "The Phil Donahue show," Mike Wallace interviews, and "The David Letterman Show."

Book:
Our Dreaming Mind

Contact Dr. Van de Castle for your taped dream interpretations, or consultation service.

—— Walden Welch ——
Astrologer

Walden Welch has been an astrologer for over thirty years. Walden knew as a child that his work as an adult would be in some area of the psychic field. When he was sixteen, Gavin Arthur predicted that he would be doing exactly that. He started out in mediumship, giving psychic readings at the early age of seventeen. Walden works from readings that Edgar Cayce gave on astrology.

Walden's emphasis is on predictions, and the accuracy for his predictions is very high. He spends a great deal of time in San Francisco doing radio and television shows, particularly "The Olan Span Show," on radio KGO.

My first meeting with Walden Welch was years ago. Before I had met Sherri Bolling, I saw him on her show "Look Who's Talking." He is Sherri's personal consultant. (Yes, even psychics have their own personal psychics!) After I had been going to Sherri for guidance, and she had gotten to know me well, I decided to see Walden, who knew nothing about me, to get new insight. I called him and had to wait four months to see him.

I was extremely impressed when he interpreted the chart that he had done for me with the information that I had supplied. Everything that he said was accurate, and he was able to discuss my life's events and the years that they happened. I was impressed, that is, until I asked about my marriage. I had just got married in April (this was November), and I was excited to be planning to finally join my husband the following

month, after living on opposite coasts since the wedding. When I asked Walden about the marriage, he described the woman that my husband was spending his time with! He also told me that the marriage would not survive. I didn't believe him. In this, however, as in all the areas that he addressed, he was correct. He told me that he always tells truth and that, when something "bad" happens, it's because something better is in store for me. My husband and I had some karma to work out, and then we had our separate ways to go. After a while I accepted the truth in everything Walden told me. (He recently did an update on my chart, and I am indeed a happy camper.)

Walden has clients who began seeing him when he was eighteen years old and continue to come to him. And now their children are coming for guidance.

Although Walden works five days a week, he has a waiting list of several months. If you are out of town, he won't make you a taped reading, but he will give you a reading over the phone by appointment. During the end of October and the first half of November, Walden is in Honolulu and is available for consultation there. He is also in New York City at various times and he travels to many different areas of the country to give lectures, giving readings wherever he is.

Judi West
Trance Channel
Expert Intuitive

When Judi was a child, she knew things that other people didn't know, saw things that other people didn't see, and heard voices that other people didn't hear. She knew that she had a great deal of protection because she made it through many unlikely circumstances. She knew that she had some kind of unusual gift and that it must be used for good and must be respected.

There wasn't any real encouragement to develop her gift until she was in her thirties. In Oregon, she met a psychiatrist (with whom she interned as a psychotherapist) who gave her some insight into her ability and began to teach her how to use it in a formal way. He sent her clients, and she began to build a network of clients who have been with her ever since. This psychiatrist taught Judi how to work under light trance. She no longer uses this method but finds it helpful for accessing another point of view. She recalled under light hypnosis that she had been an intuitive back in 1700 B.C. and had done that kind of work all her life. This memory enabled her to use past knowledge to enhance her abilities.

The area of work that Judi most enjoys is developing scientific technology and working with precise and exact prediction. Personal consultation is a small portion of what she does. She does small business consultations, personnel work and problem solving, and scientific problem solving. She also helps businesses in planning processes that are difficult to predict and gives insights into the past, present, and future in a way that maximizes a company's potential and current opportunities. Judi enjoys working with a variety of people, in art, science, medicine, law, and administration, among others. What she loves most is the opportunity to open windows into areas of life that she doesn't ordinarily experience.

Judi does visualization work, identifying from a distance what something looks like, how to find somebody or something according to its name or location. She finds lost items, describes people (including what they will look like in the future) and how a client will meet them and the impact they'll have in the client's life.

For four years, when she worked with the psychiatrist, they recorded and evaluated consultations, some of which was predictive, with clients. He estimated that her accuracy rate was 97-98 percent. Judi also gets reports back from clients telling her how accurate her predictions are. She tries to be as precise as she can and stays away from vague predictions or predictions that would be hard to prove.

She feels that this is a very important time in history and that what we put in motion now will create a reality for a long time. It's important that we be very clear about our values, our intentions, and how we design the future. She believes that we need to develop the attitude and skill to use valuable knowledge from the past for the benefit of everyone.

Since 1974, Judi has been working through the personality of Osamara, the Egyptian priestess.

William H. Kautz and Melanie Branon, in the national reference guide of their book *Channeling, the Intuitive Connection*, list her as the only expert channel in the southwest. Judi lives in Santa Fe with her husband Randall, a professional photographer.

Judi has written several books:
Personal Growth Training Questionnaire and Handbook gives guidelines for evaluation of readiness for transforma-

tional practices. It is designed for both students and teachers.

Rose-A-Down Dilly is about the folly of forced transformation on a beloved.

The Brothers, channeled from survivors of the Black Death in the British Isles, is an account of the ancient history as well as the future of Britain. The book has been written as a screenplay as well and is also available on tape.

—— Zolar ——
(Dr. Donald Papon)
Astrologer
Homeopath
Educator
Author

The name *Zolar* is actually a trademark created by Bruce King back during the Great Depression. King patterned himself after a European astrologer named Kobar and went onto sell Zolar products. Dr. Donald Papon worked with Zolar—King—in the publishing field, and when King and his wife died they left the Zolar trademark to Dr. Papon, who continues to add to the lengthy list of books that are published under the Zolar name. (In 1977, I bought my first dream book, *Zolar's Encyclopedia and Dictionary of Dreams*, which, tattered and held together by a rubber band, still has a place beside my bed.)

The current Zolar, Dr. Papon, is a walking encyclopedia of metaphysics. His beginnings in the field go back to childhood. At age twelve, he discovered that he could put people into hypnotic states; he did so at school and was expelled. Soon after, one of his classmates saw a book he was carrying and suggested that he meet his father, who was a master in a secret order that dealt in metaphysics and who was an extraordinary healer. As a freshman in high school, Donald went to his parents to receive permission to begin studying with the order. There in the Bronx, this group taught spiritual healing and surveyed all of the mystical arts; their main thrust was to develop psychic abilities.

At age twenty-four, he became an ordained minister at the Church of Divine Metaphysics and founded and pastored a church, The Church of Healing Hand, in Red Bank, New Jersey.

When Dr. Papon went to college he majored in philosophy, then studied law. From there he studied holistic health and homeopathy as a result of a Jungian analysis with Erlo Van Waveren, a direct disciple of Carl Jung. Dr. Papon considered becoming a Jungian analyst, but he began having dreams of healing in another lifetime, catapulting him to the study and practice of homeopathy. Meanwhile, he had been pursuing astrology for twenty years and had quite a following in New York. He also taught the first classes in astrology that were offered for credit in the United States at The New School for Social Research. He also opened a school, Academy of Mystic Arts, and he eventually compiled his lesson plans into book form. His books are how-to books, in response to what he sees is a desire for people to take back their power and learn how balance themselves in body, mind, and spirit. In addition to all these enterprises, he published a number of astrological magazines and worked closely with the original Zolar during the depression, sold horoscopes to Woolworth's, was on the radio, and built the foundations of what we might call popular astrology.

To return to Donald Papon's dream—he dreamed that he had to choose between astrology and homeopathy and chose homeopathy. The next morning he called a friend to see if he wanted to buy his astrology practice.

Dr. Papon practices homeopathy in New York City. It was there that he met Dr. Wallace F. (Dr. Mac) MacNaughton, who worked with colour, homeopathy, and radionics for more than sixty years. Dr. Mac served as a friend and mentor until his death in 1982 and influenced Dr. Papon's use of colour therapy.

Dr. Papon is affiliated with The New School, Hunter College, Bronx Community College, and Brookdale Community

College. He is also the founder and president of the International Homeopathic Alliance, Ltd., which consists of homeopaths from all over the world. He spends his time writing and in homeopathic research, and he serves as a consultant in homeopathy, colour therapy, and radionics. He is still an astrologer, but he focuses his interest on the medical area of the astrological chart.

As a homeopath, Dr. Papon works with more than two thousand remedies. Using a radionic device, he can measure your electromagnetic field and learn about your illness, whether it be physical, mental, or emotional. He prescribes remedies which he manufactures himself with state-of-the-art equipment from Europe. He uses astrology to help him be more exact about possibilities. For example, three people may come to him with pneumonia, and he would give all three different remedies because they are all different people.

After meeting with Zolar, I sent him a handwritten note. He called shortly thereafter and joked that I should never send a handwritten correspondence to one such as he because it will be analyzed. I was grateful that he had done so, because, using his radionic device on my handwriting, he had determined that I had a parasite which causes symptoms of arthritis, a slow metabolism, miscarriages, bad memory, and other ailments. I had suffered from all of the symptoms he mentioned; according to Dr. Papon, I must have had the parasite for years, which explains so many things in my life. The Doc sent me some homeopathic remedies, and within a week I had more energy, the simple things in life were no longer a chore, and I even lost ten pounds. Another of the many benefits I have gained from project—not only do I now have a homeopathic physician, but I also have a new friend who truly cares about others.

Zolar/Dr. Papon travels all over the world giving lectures.

Books that are available:
Zolar's Book of Dreams, Numbers and Lucky Days

Zolar's Book of Spirits
*— Zolar's Compendium of Occult Theories and
    Practices*
*⤳ Zolar's Encyclopedia of Ancient and Forbidden
    Knowledge*
Zolar's Encyclopedia and Dictionary of Dreams
*Zolar's Encyclopedia of Omens, Signs and
    Superstitions*
Zolar's Star Mates
Zolar's—It's All in the Stars
⤳ Zolar's Mastermind Consciousness
Zolar's High Magick
Dancing Heart To Heart
Zolar's Magick of Color
Forever Together (Reincarnation)

—— Robert Zoller ——
Astrologer
Alchemist

Robert Zoller, who approaches astrology in a very scientific way, is a master at what he does. I met with Robert in his New York City apartment; he had my astrological chart prepared, and within about ten minutes he told me where I have been, where I am now, and what lies ahead for me. He amazed me with the amount of information he was able to provide in such a short time. I didn't even get a chance to ask him any questions—he had answered them before I asked. He also looked at my hands with a magnifying glass and told me in a few short minutes why I am the person that I am, what went on in my childhood, and what will be going on in the next few years.

Robert Zoller became interested in astrology in 1969, when he was fifteen or sixteen. He also studied other avenues, such as tarot cards, but he chose astrology because it gave him a way of dealing with time and other approaches. Astrology also appealed to him because it could be handled in a rather intellectual and analytical manner, rather than as psychic phenomenon. Although psychic abilities with astrology can give tremendous detailed insights, he feels that, for himself, they are not reliable. He prefers handling it as a set of algebraic symbols.

In 1970, he began studying astrology through the writings of Zolton Mason, a medieval astrologer.

In 1974 he took up the study of Latin so that he could

better research astrology. In 1975 he began translating and has been working professionally as an astrologer since 1976. Clients from all over the world call on Robert for astrological counsel. Most of his clients check in, so to speak, once a year for an update; they also call with specific questions about situations in their lives.

Robert is a scholar as well as an astrologer. In 1980 he published his book *The Arabic Parts In Astrology: A Lost Key To Prediction*. The book is a translation of the twelfth-century Latin astrological text of Guido Bonatti, *Liber Astronomicus*. Dealing with the same material, Robert also works with Rob Hand and Bob Schmidt on Project Hindsight, which they began at the United Astrological Conference a couple of years ago. This project involves translating ancient texts monthly—Schmidt translates from the Greek and Robert from the Latin—and offering the translations to the astrological community. The material is available by subscription—sort of an ancient-book-of-the-month club—or as individual books. The project was born of the realization that until now astrology has been dominated in the English-speaking world by people with limited access to ancient material; they go in their individual directions and therefore tradition is lost. By making the ancient texts available, these men provide an opportunity to assimilate the old with new knowledge.

Robert Zoller studied Latin and history at the Institute of Medieval and Renaissance Studies. He is on the faculty of The Open Center of New York, the American Federation of Astrologers, and the National Council for Geocosmic Research.

When I asked him about his lectures, he printed a list out on his computer—sixteen pages long. So I encourage you to contact him for information about available lectures and classes. A small sample of his lectures follows:

Arabic Astrology
Jewish Astrology
Renaissance Occultism

Pythagoreanism and Magic
Hermeticism: Astrology—Alchemy—Magic
Plato, Aristotle, and Astrology

Directory

*You've read about them and seen photographs of them,
and now here's how you can get to know them.*

And May the Force Be With You!

Kenna Akash
P.O. Box 335
Sedona, Arizona 86340
602-282-0207

Lynn Andrews
2934½ Beverly Glen Circle
Los Angeles, California 90077
800-726-0082

Sherri Evans Bolling
10235 Fair Oaks Blvd. #202
Fair Oaks, California 95628
916-967-4064

Celeste
P.O. Box 4044
Sedona, Arizona 86339
602-282-1294

Sandra Dolan
22 Elmont Rd.
Trenton, New Jersey 08610
609-585-9575

Elaine Eagle Woman
P.O. Box 392
Sedona, Arizona 86336
602-284-0210

Patricia Hayes
DELPHI
P.O. Box 70
Silver Mine Road
McCaysville, Georgia 30555
706-492-2772

Jananda
P.O. Box 4044
Sedona, Arizona 86339
602-282-1294

Kathy Lawrance
P.O. Box 2853
Sedona, Arizona 86339
602-282-3014

William Lawrance
P.O. Box 2853
Sedona, Arizona 86339
602-634-1210

Jeanie Loomis
116 Montowese St.
Branford, Connecticut 06405
203-481-6091

Lin David Martin
P.O. Box 2063
Sedona, Arizona 86339
602-282-0260

Robin Miller
P.O. Box 534
Sedona, Arizona 86339

Robert Monroe
The Monroe Institute
Route 1, Box 175
Faber, Virginia 22938-9749
804-361-1252

Kathy Oddenino
133 A Lee Drive
Annapolis, Maryland 21403
410-268-3752

Rinatta Paries
P.O. Box 242
La Jolla, California 92038
619-551-1210

Foster Perry
Aymara Foundation
14 Alondra Rd.
Santa Fe, New Mexico 87505
505-988-4022

Sally Perry
P.O. Box 4870
Virginia Beach, Virginia 23454
804-481-5489

Mary Reagan
P.O. Box 905
Sedona, Arizona 86339
602-282-7947

Pat Rodegast
7568 San Miguel Way
Naples, Florida 33942
813-594-0501

Kevin Ryerson
P.O. Box 151080
San Rafael, California 94915
415-454-9727

Mother Sarita
3126 Biggs St.
National City, California 91950
619-470-2510

Gordon-Michael Scallion
Matrix Institute
RR1, Box 391
Westmoreland, New Hampshire 03467
603-399-4916

Sandi Staylor
P.O. Box 1218
Newport News, Virginia 23601
804-595-2170

Dr. Robert Van de Castle
P.O. Box 3048
University Station
Charlottesville, Virginia 22903
804-984-0570

Walden Welch
P.O. Box 818
Boyes Hot Springs, California 95446
707-996-8226

Judi West
P.O. Box 9837
Santa Fe, New Mexico 87504
505-473-9754

Zolar (Donald Papon)
236 State Street
Princeton, New Jersey 08540-1312
212-505-2481

Robert Zoller
170 Cedar Street
Cliffside, New Jersey 07010
201-945-6189

—— About the Author ——

Loretta R. Washburn was born September 20, 1951, in Oakland, California. Her life as an internationally-acclaimed photographer has put her work in galleries and museums all over the world as well as in art books and magazines.

She has also done a great deal of psychic work, including psychic investigation, teaching metaphysics, and intuitive counseling.

Loretta is the mother of three lovely daughters and resides in Virginia Beach, Virginia, where she devotes her life to her children and her career.